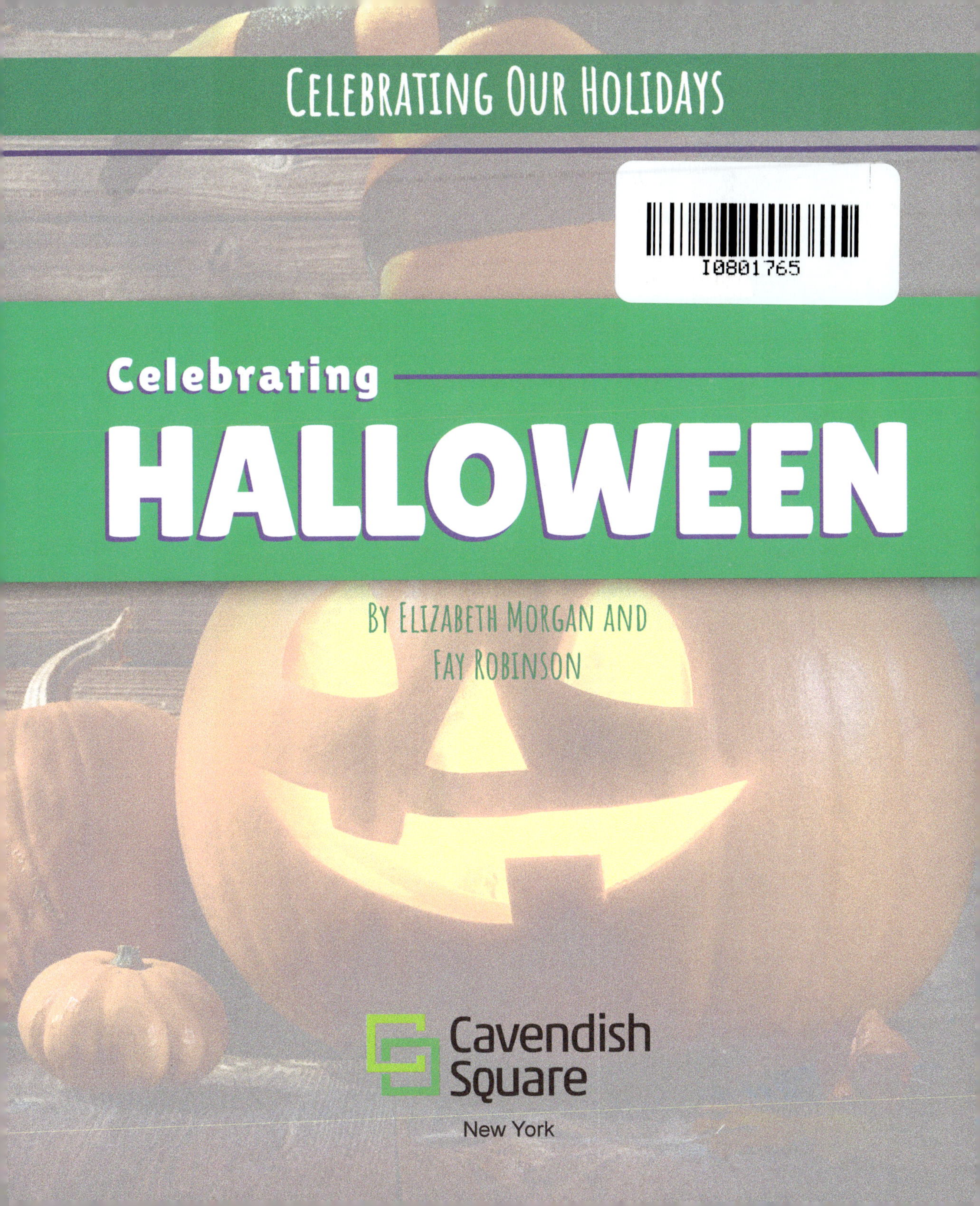

Celebrating Our Holidays

Celebrating HALLOWEEN

By Elizabeth Morgan and
Fay Robinson

Cavendish Square
New York

Published in 2023 by Cavendish Square Publishing, LLC
29 E. 21st Street New York, NY 10010

Website: cavendishsq.com

Library of Congress Cataloging-in-Publication Data

Names: Morgan, Elizabeth, author. | Robinson, Fay, author.
Title: Celebrating Halloween / Elizabeth Morgan, Fay Robinson.
Description: New York : Cavendish Square Publishing, [2023] | Series: Celebrating Our Holidays | "Portions of this work were originally authored by Fay Robinson and published as Halloween: Costumes and Treats on All Hallows' Eve. All new material this edition authored by Elizabeth Morgan"–Copyright page.
Identifiers: LCCN 2021047525 | ISBN 9781502665010 (Set) | ISBN 9781502665027 (Library Binding) | ISBN 9781502665003 (Paperback) | ISBN 9781502665034 (eBook)
Subjects: LCSH: Halloween–Juvenile literature.
Classification: LCC GT4965 .M6644 2023 | DDC 394.2646–dc23/eng/20211130
LC record available at https://lccn.loc.gov/2021047525

Editor: Katie Kawa
Copyeditor: Jill Keppeler
Designer: Deanna Paternostro

The photographs in this book are used by permission and through the courtesy of: Cover p. 1 Alexander Raths/Shutterstock.com; back cover pp. 3, 5 7, 9, 10, 15, 17, 19, 21, 23, 27, 28, 29, 30, 31, 32 N.D.Vector/Shutterstock.com; p. 4 Daniel jakulovic/Shutterstock.com; p. 6 Enfi/Shutterstock.com; p. 8 Svet_Feo/Shutterstock.com; p. 11 Raffa Thildinlooke/Shutterstock.com; p. 12 K.A.Willis/Shutterstock.com; p. 14 Zabotnova Inna/Shutterstock.com; p. 16 praszkiewicz/Shutterstock.com; pp. 17, 22 Sean Locke Photography/Shutterstock.com; p. 18 Teri Virbickis/Shutterstock.com; p. 20 Yuganov Konstantin/Shutterstock.com; p. 21 Anna Kraynova/Shutterstock.com; p. 25 Kristen Prahl/Shutterstock.com; p. 26 Monkey Business Images/Shutterstock.com; p. 28 stockcreations/Shutterstock.com.

CPSIA compliance information: Batch #CSCSQ23: For further information contact Cavendish Square Publishing LLC, New York, New York, at 1-877-980-4450.

Printed in the United States of America

CONTENTS

Every holiday has its own special activities. On Halloween, kids often go trick-or-treating!

CHAPTER ONE

TRICK OR TREAT!

Every year on October 31, the same three words can be heard in small neighborhoods, big cities, and even busy apartment buildings across the United States: "Trick or treat!" They're said by kids dressed up as witches, ghosts, princesses, superheroes, and almost anything else you can imagine. Those words mean it's Halloween—a day of costumes, candy, and all things creepy.

HALLOWEEN HISTORY

Halloween is one of the most popular holidays people celebrate today. Adults celebrate it. Kids celebrate it. People from many different backgrounds celebrate it. However, do they know what they're really celebrating?

The history of Halloween isn't as well known as the history of other holidays such as Christmas, Hanukkah, or Thanksgiving. However, that doesn't mean Halloween is a brand-new holiday or one without an important past. In fact, the history of Halloween goes back thousands of years. Some of the **traditions** we love today, including trick-or-treating, have their roots in ancient times.

Halloween happens in the fall. In the Northern Hemisphere, or half of Earth, this is the time of year when days get shorter and the weather gets colder. Today, we know why this happens, but ancient peoples couldn't explain it. It scared them.

THE SCIENCE OF SHORTER DAYS

Halloween happens at a time of year when the days get shorter for half of the world. It gets darker earlier and stays dark longer. This is because the Northern Hemisphere is tilted, or tipped, away from the sun during this time of year. The longest day of the year is in June, when summer starts. The shortest day of the year is in December, when winter starts.

FUN IN THE FALL

Understanding the history of Halloween begins with understanding how ancient peoples viewed the season of fall. Today, it's many people's favorite season—and not just because it's when Halloween happens. Fall is a time for eating pumpkin-flavored treats, watching football, and jumping in piles of colorful leaves.

In the past, though, fall was often seen as a scary time. It seemed like everything was ending as the leaves fell from the trees and many plants died. It got darker earlier in some parts of the world, and the weather got colder. This cold weather could be dangerous, or unsafe, for ancient peoples.

People sometimes enjoy scaring each other—and being scared—on Halloween today. However, in the past, the fear people felt at this time of year wasn't fun. To learn the whole scary story, we have to travel far back in time!

Many of today's Halloween traditions, including telling scary stories, have been around for thousands of years.

CHAPTER TWO

ANCIENT CELEBRATIONS

Halloween is a day when people wear costumes, tell scary stories, and bob for apples at parties. These traditions can be traced back to two important ancient groups: the Celts and the Romans. Their beliefs and festivals, or gatherings for important days, played a big part in the history of Halloween.

THE CELTIC NEW YEAR

The Celts (also spelled "Kelts") lived in what's now Europe, especially today's Great Britain, Ireland, and northern France, more than 2,000 years ago. They believed in many gods. Some of the gods were good, and some were evil. The Celts told stories about the gods to make sense of things they couldn't understand, such as the changing seasons.

Why did the sun seem to go away as winter came? Would the sun's light come back? The early Celts weren't sure. Fall and winter were scary times of the year, and the Celts took time to honor their gods in the hopes of surviving, or making it through, the period of darkness and cold after the warm and sunny days of summer.

One important Celtic festival that still takes place in the fall is Samhain. It marks the end of summer and the harvest season, which is when crops are collected. Samhain was seen as the start of a new year for the ancient Celts. This new year began on November 1, according to calendars used today.

Today's New Year's holiday is often seen as a time to think about the future, and Samhain was no different. In fact, the Celts believed this was a great time to hear **predictions** about the future. During Samhain, the ancient Celts believed the world of humans and the world of gods and spirits weren't separated the way they were the rest of the year. This made it easier for spirits to show druids, who were like Celtic priests, the future.

A Spooky Night

The lack of separation between the spirit world and the human world on Samhain didn't just make it easier to predict the future. The Celts believed it also made it easier for spirits to cause problems for the living. This was especially true on the Celtic **version** of New Year's Eve—October 31. On this night, Celts believed the spirits of the dead could return to Earth. These ghosts were said to visit their old homes, but this wasn't always seen as a friendly **reunion**.

Samhain Today

Samhain isn't just an ancient holiday that led to Halloween. It's still celebrated by people around the world today. It's a popular holiday for those who practice Wicca, which is a modern **pagan** religion, or belief system, often connected with the natural world. This festival is still celebrated from October 31 to November 1 and still includes the traditional fires that were a major part of the holiday in ancient times.

The Celts were afraid of what the ghosts and evil spirits might do on October 31. They built huge outdoor fires, called bonfires, to keep the ghosts away. They offered sacrifices—animals or crops given as gifts to the gods—that they burned in the fires to make the gods happy. People sometimes wore costumes made of animal skins during this **ritual**. Some say the costumes were worn to make it harder for the evil spirits to recognize the Celts.

The belief in evil spirits made it easier for people to play tricks on each other on this night and blame it on the ghosts. There might not have been the kind of treats we have today on October 31, but Samhain might be where the Halloween tradition of tricks began.

Fire was an important part of Samhain celebrations, and bonfires are still a popular fall event today.

Celebrating with the Romans

Halloween also has some connection to ancient Roman festivals. During the first century CE, the Romans took over many lands controlled by the Celts. The Romans, like the Celts, believed in many gods. One was Pomona—the goddess of fruit trees and orchards, which is where apples are grown. Around November 1, the Romans

Shown here is a statue of the Roman goddess Pomona. Like the Celts and many other ancient peoples, the Romans told stories of gods and goddesses to explain natural events they couldn't understand, such as the seasons and the success or failure of a harvest.

celebrated Pomona with a festival. Because Pomona is connected to apples, some historians believe the Halloween tradition of bobbing for apples—dunking your head in water to grab apples with your teeth—can be traced back to this festival.

The Roman festival of Feralia honored the dead. It was held in late October. This is another ancient festival that historians believe **influenced** our modern Halloween celebrations. Although Samhain, Feralia, and the celebrations for Pomona all played a part in creating the holiday we celebrate today, it would take many more years—and the influence of many other groups—before Halloween as we know it now began to take shape.

The Roman Catholic Church got its name because it's centered in Rome. It became the official religion of the Roman Empire in 380 CE. Shown here is St. Peter's Basilica, which is an important church in Vatican City—the center of the Catholic faith. It's an indepedent state surrounded by the city of Rome, Italy.

CHAPTER THREE

THE CATHOLIC INFLUENCE

Samhain and the ancient Roman festivals were pagan celebrations. Over time, ancient Rome moved away from pagan beliefs, and many Romans began to follow a religion known as Christianity, which is based on the teachings of Jesus Christ.

The Catholic Church—also known as the Roman Catholic Church—was one of the first official Christian churches. It influenced the lives of its followers in many ways, including the festivals they celebrated. In fact, two important Catholic holy days played a part in the **development** of Halloween from its pagan past to the holiday we celebrate today.

ALL SAINTS' DAY

One important aspect, or part, of the Catholic faith is the belief in saints, or special people honored for their holy lives after they've died. The Roman Catholic Church created All Saints' Day to honor these saints. It was first celebrated by many Catholics in the spring, around Easter. The church later changed the date to November 1.

Historians believe November 1 was chosen as All Saints' Day because Catholic leaders wanted to stop celebrations of Samhain. This festival was still celebrated by people with Celtic backgrounds. However, the Catholic Church didn't like Samhain because it was a pagan holiday. The church wanted to replace Samhain with a

Catholic holiday. They also called their new holiday All Hallows' Day, meaning "all saints." The night before was called All Hallows' Eve. This was eventually shortened to Halloween—the name we use for October 31 today.

Going Souling

Later, the Catholic Church made November 2 a holy day too. It's called All Souls' Day. On this day, the souls of all the dead are remembered—not just those of the saints.

On the night before All Souls' Day in England, the poor went door to door singing and begging for food at each home. Families would give out money or special round cakes called soul cakes. In return, the poor promised to pray for any of their family members who had died. This activity was called going souling. Some people went souling on both the night before All Souls' Day and the night before All Saints' Day, or All Hallows' Eve.

A Blend of Cultures and Celebrations

Although the Catholic Church tried to stop celebrations of pagan holidays, one look at modern Halloween traditions shows that it wasn't entirely successful. Although the name of the holiday and the practice

All Saints' Day and All Souls' Day are still celebrated by Catholics around the world today. These days are often spent at church or visiting the graves of loved ones who've died.

An All Souls' Day Treat

Soul cakes were an important part of All Souls' Day traditions in England. Although people don't go souling anymore, there are still plenty of recipes for soul cakes that people can bake and share at this time of year. There are many different ways to make soul cakes—some are more like tiny cakes, while others are more like a cookie or a biscuit. In addition, they come in different shapes, and some are even marked with a cross—a traditional symbol, or sign, of the Christian faith.

of trick-or-treating seem to have their roots in All Hallows' Eve and the Catholic practice of going souling, many other parts of the holiday still come from the Celts and Romans.

In the United States, Halloween took on its own special style thanks to the many different groups of people who settled there. It took time for this day to catch on across the country, but now, most Americans—especially American children—look forward to this holiday and all the spooky and silly ways we celebrate it.

Today's Halloween celebrations are a mix of Catholic and pagan traditions, with plenty of modern fun mixed in too!

One of the most common Halloween decorations is the jack-o'-lantern, which is a carved pumpkin that sometimes has a light inside.

CHAPTER FOUR

Symbols of the Season

When you walk around your neighborhood on Halloween night, you might see jack-o'-lanterns with creepy faces. If you watch a Halloween movie with your friends, it might show witches casting spooky spells. Even the words "trick or treat" are symbols of this holiday. Where did some of the most popular Halloween symbols come from? Keep reading to find out!

Jack of the Lantern

Carving pumpkins is something many people do to get ready for Halloween. This is a way to make jack-o'-lanterns. There are a number of stories behind this symbol. According to an Irish story, Jack was a very bad man who played a trick on the devil. When he died, he couldn't get into heaven, but the devil didn't want him either. Instead, Jack was forced to walk around the earth in darkness forever, without a resting place. When Jack complained that he couldn't see in the dark, the devil gave him a glowing coal. Jack placed the coal in a turnip and used it to light the way. The story says that poor Jack is still wandering the earth today. He's known as "Jack of the Lantern," or "Jack O'Lantern," because a lantern is a kind of light.

The Irish put coals inside turnips or potatoes on Halloween just like Jack in the story. They carved scary faces on the vegetables. When the Irish came to America, they used pumpkins, which were easier to carve than turnips. Today, we do the same thing. With a flashlight or another kind of light inside, the pumpkin glows just like a lantern.

Witches of the Past and Present

Witches are a popular part of Halloween today. Long ago, however, people were very afraid of witches. People thought they could cast spells to make others sick or turn them into animals. People also thought the witches could turn themselves into animals. People blamed witches for bad things they couldn't explain. Sometimes they called women witches for not following the rules or acting in ways they didn't like.

Today, there are still people who call themselves witches, but they're nothing like the figures from scary stories. They're not bad. They just have their own beliefs and often follow the religion known as Wicca. Many of these people still celebrate Samhain.

Witches are a symbol of Halloween, but they can also be real people. In the past, women could be killed if someone thought they were witches. Today, witches can celebrate their Wiccan beliefs freely in the United States.

The Trick-or-Treating Tradition

The most famous Halloween tradition is trick-or-treating, but where did it come from? One explanation comes from Samhain. To keep the spirits of the dead

No More Tricks

For a time in the 1920s and 1930s, Halloween tricks became less fun and more dangerous. Young people sometimes used this holiday to commit acts of vandalism—destroying other people's property. In some cases, Halloween even became a night for violence. Over the years, communities pushed to make this holiday safer for everyone. Today, Halloween is seen as a holiday that's much more about treats than tricks.

happy, the Celts put out offerings of food for them. In some cases, this food was later given to the poor.

Other stories, some from the Celts, tell that people believed that dressing in costumes would confuse or drive away unwelcome spirits or ghosts. During the Middle Ages, people would also go mumming, which means they'd dress up in scary costumes and perform for treats. Guising, which happened in Scotland and some other places, was a similar tradition.

No matter how it started, going door to door for Halloween treats became popular across America by the 1920s and 1930s. However, it took until at least the 1940s for people to actually start using the words "trick or treat." Throughout history, people sometimes used Halloween as a day to play tricks on others, but today, treats are much more likely—and much nicer to share.

The tradition of wearing costumes while trick-or-treating can also be traced back to the Celts.

Halloween is fun to celebrate with friends!

CHAPTER FIVE

Having Fun and Staying Safe

Being a little scared on Halloween can be fun. It's why people visit haunted houses, wear creepy costumes, and watch scary movies. However, it's important to be safe as you celebrate this holiday too. That's the best way to keep the fear all in good fun.

Creative Costumes

The Celts of long ago wore costumes to mark Samhain. Today, kids and adults still wear costumes on October 31. Like the Celts, some people want their costumes to be scary. Many people dress up as ghosts, skeletons, witches, or zombies.

The costumes don't have to be scary, though. Funny or pretty costumes or costumes based on favorite characters are good also. Some people are princesses for Halloween, while others are firefighters. You might want to dress up like a superhero or an animal you love. Costumes can be handmade or store-bought, and both can look great! It's fun to look at everyone's costumes on Halloween.

Spooky Celebrations

Trick-or-treating may be the most famous way people celebrate Halloween, but people celebrate in other ways too. Some people, especially adults, enjoy answering the door for trick-or-treaters. They get dressed up to hand out candy. Sometimes their pets will be dressed up too!

Some schools have Halloween parades. Children get to show off their costumes in front of a crowd. Other schools and communities might have a Halloween dance. Some towns have pumpkin contests—perhaps for the biggest pumpkin or the coolest carving. Other towns have scarecrow festivals. People put out scarecrows they make for everyone to see.

Some communities have haunted houses for people to visit. These might be fun for people of all ages or so scary they're just for adults. It's important to know what kind of haunted house you're visiting before you go.

Halloween parties are fun too. There might be apple cider, hot cocoa, and different foods made from apples or pumpkins, such as breads, pies, and other treats. People can wear their costumes, listen to Halloween music, and watch Halloween movies.

Halloween Safety

Halloween frights are often fun, but people should still be careful when they go out on Halloween night. Here are some safety tips for trick-or-treating:

- Young children should always go trick-or-treating with a trusted adult.
- Stay on well-lit streets, cross only at corners, and stay on the sidewalks if possible.

Haunted houses can be a fun part of Halloween, but not everyone likes them—and that's OK. People should only celebrate Halloween in a way that feels safe and good for them.

- Put reflective tape on your costume so drivers can see you in the dark.
- If you wear a mask, make sure you can see out of it clearly.
- Have an adult at home check your treats before eating them.

If you have any food allergies, it's important to ask an adult if it's safe to eat something at a Halloween party or after trick-or-treating.

Types of Treats

The most popular Halloween treat is candy, and people buy and eat a lot of it! In fact, it's been reported that Americans spend more than $2 billion on Halloween candy every year. However, some other Halloween treats include stickers, small toys, plastic jewelry, pencil erasers, and slime. These are often great treats for kids who can't eat candy because of food allergies.

Happy Halloween!

Whether you go to a haunted house, throw a Halloween party, or go trick-or-treating around your neighborhood, there are plenty of ways to have fun on Halloween. This holiday has been around for a long time, and it only seems to be getting more popular as time goes on. From the ancient Celts to today's trick-or-treaters, people love to find ways to have a frightfully fun fall. What's your favorite part of Halloween?

HOLIDAY HOW-TO

MAKE YOUR OWN MUMMY HOT DOGS

INGREDIENTS:

1 can (8 ounces) of crescent roll dough

3 slices of American cheese

12 hot dogs

2 tablespoons of butter, melted

yellow mustard

Ask an adult to help you make these spooky snacks for your next Halloween party!

Directions:

1. Preheat the oven to 375°F (191°C).
2. Line a baking sheet with parchment paper.
3. Separate the crescent roll dough into 4 rectangles, and cut each rectangle into thin strips.
4. Cut each slice of American cheese into 4 strips.
5. Place 1 hot dog on top of a strip of cheese.
6. Wrap strips of crescent roll dough around the hot dog and cheese to look like bandages. You'll need about 4 strips of dough for each hot dog.
7. Place the hot dog, cheese side down, on the baking sheet, and brush with melted butter.
8. Repeat steps 5–7 for the rest of the hot dogs.
9. Bake for 12–15 minutes, until the dough is golden brown.
10. Using a toothpick, dot mustard onto each hot dog for eyes.

GLOSSARY

allergy: A condition that produces a bad bodily reaction to certain foods, animals, or surroundings.

development: The act or process of growing or causing something to become more advanced.

influence: To have an effect on the condition or development of something.

pagan: Relating to the worship of many gods and goddesses or the earth or nature.

prediction: A statement about what might or will happen in the future.

reunion: The act of people coming together again after they have been apart.

ritual: A religious ceremony, especially one consisting of a series of actions performed in a certain order.

tradition: A way of thinking, behaving, or doing something that's been used by people in a particular society for a long time.

version: A form of something that is different from others.

FIND OUT MORE

Books

Markovics, Pearl. *Halloween*. Minneapolis, MN: Bearport Publishing, 2019.

Meinking, Mary. *Make Frightful Props: DIY Eyeballs, Organs, and More*. North Mankato, MN: Capstone Press, 2019.

Shofner, Melissa Raé. *The Story Behind Halloween*. New York, NY: PowerKids Press, 2020.

Websites

All About the Spookiest Holiday—Halloween!
www.cbc.ca/kidscbc2/the-feed/whats-the-story-halloween
This website features colorful Halloween photos and fun facts about the history of this holiday.

Playing It Safe on Halloween
kidshealth.org/en/kids/halloween-safety.html
Halloween can be a fun holiday, but only if it's celebrated safely. This website breaks down important safety tips to help you have a safe and happy Halloween.

Publisher's note to educators and parents: Our editors have carefully reviewed these websites to ensure that they are suitable for students. Many websites change frequently, however, and we cannot guarantee that a site's future contents will continue to meet our high standards of quality and educational value. Be advised that students should be closely supervised whenever they access the Internet.

INDEX